Fact Finders®

Awesome ENGiNEERiNG

SPACECRAFT

SALLY SPRAY

WITH ARTWORK BY MARK RUFFLE

CAPSTONE PRESS
a capstone imprint

Fact Finders Books are published by Capstone Press,
1710 Roe Crest Drive, North Mankato, Minnesota 56003
www.mycapstone.com

Library of Congress Cataloging-in-Publication Data
Library of Congress Cataloging-in-Publication data is available on the Library of Congress website.

978-1-5435-1337-0 (library binding)
978-1-5435-1343-1 (paperback)

Editorial Credits

Series editor: Paul Rockett
Series design and illustration: Mark Ruffle
www.rufflebrothers.com
Consultant:
Andrew Woodward BEng (Hons) CEng MICE FCIArb

Photo Credits

Aniza/Dreamstime: 28cl. Azat1976/Shutterstock: 23b. Goran Cakmazovic/Shutterstock: 8b. ESB Professional/Shutterstock: 18t. estherspoon/Shutterstock: 28r. Everett Historical/Shutterstock: 11t. Julien Hautcoeur/Shutterstock: 13b. Philip Lange/Shutterstock: 20t. Jianhua Liang/Dreamstime: 29tc. Mandritoiu/Dreamstime: 5. Mikhail Markovskiy/Shutterstock: 29tr. Shaiful Zamri Masri/Dreamstime: 28c. George Rinhart/Corbis Historical/Getty Images: 6. TonyV3112/Shutterstock: 26. Konstantin Tronin/Shutterstock: 25cr. Thor Jorgen Udvang/Shutterstock: 29tl. Tao Chuen Yeh/AFP/Getty Images: 18b.

First published in Great Britain in 2017
by The Watts Publishing Group
Copyright © The Watts Publishing Group, 2017

Printed and bound in China.
010755S18

TABLE OF CONTENTS

3, 2, 1, BLAST OFF!

People have been dreaming of space travel for hundreds of years. But only in the last century has our **technology** and engineering been advanced enough to build spacecraft that can blast off into the night sky—exploring our **galaxy** and beyond!

WHAT IS A SPACECRAFT?

Spacecraft can be anything made by humans that is sent into space to carry out a task. They can be simple **communication satellites** that send information to us from around the world. They can also be manned vehicles and stations where people can live.

Essential features include a power source, engine, **thrusters** to change direction, a computer, and antennae for sending and receiving messages from Earth.

Computer

Thruster

Solar cells

Antenna

4

TIMELINE OF SPACECRAFT

1957

1958

1961

Russia launches the first satellite, Sputnik 1, into space (see pages 6–7).

1962

1969

A Saturn V rocket blasts Neil Armstrong and Buzz Aldrin into space on a mission that makes them the first humans to walk on the moon (see pages 10–11).

1971

1977

Voyager 1 and Voyager 2 are launched into space. They are the furthest traveled spacecraft at the time (see pages 14–15).

1981

Construction begins on the International Space Station (ISS).

1990

In 2000, the first astronauts from the United States and Russia begin living on board (see pages 22–23).

1998

*The extraordinary Wilkinson **Microwave** Anisotropy Probe (WMAP) spacecraft is launched to scan space and unlock the secrets of how and when the Universe began (see pages 24–25).*

2001

2003

Planetary rover vehicles named Spirit and Opportunity leave for Mars on their mission to explore the planet closest to Earth (see pages 26–27).

2004

2035

NASA (North American Space Agency) is formed to research flight and spaceflight.

Yuri Gagarin becomes the first man to orbit Earth in Vostok 1 (see pages 8–9).

The Apollo *lunar* roving vehicle explores the moon (see pages 12–13).

The reusable space shuttle takes its first flight (see pages 16–17). Previously, rockets had only been able to leave Earth once.

The Hubble Space Telescope is launched (see pages 18–19).

The Rosetta probe sets off to reach *comet* 67P/Churyumov-Gerasimenko. It finally reaches its target in 2014 (see pages 20–21).

Around 2035, humans expect to have a spacecraft that can take them to Mars.

SPACE AGENCIES

A space agency is a government-funded program bringing together some of the best and brightest minds to plan and accomplish space missions. Today, over 70 countries have space agencies, the most famous being NASA. Space agencies often work together, sharing expertise and information. The Cassini-Huygens mission to Saturn, launched in 1997, involved 260 scientists from 17 countries, as well as thousands of other experts that took part in the design, engineering, flying, and data collection.

IN ORBIT

An orbit is the path that an object follows around another object in space, over and over again. Objects in space that orbit around other objects are called satellites. They can be natural or artificial. They stay in orbit because of the effect of **gravity**. Gravity is an invisible force between objects that pulls objects toward each other.

Gravity keeps a satellite in orbit by pulling it toward Earth. Because the satellite is moving sideways very fast, it does not fall to Earth and instead falls into a circular path (orbit) around Earth. In effect, satellites are constantly falling around and around Earth, until they slow down when gravity pulls them to Earth.

SPUTNIK 1

The first spacecraft to orbit Earth was a tiny silver satellite called *Sputnik 1*. It orbited Earth for three months in 1957, emitting a "beep, beep" signal.

*Sputnik 1 was **spherical**, like a planet. It measured 23 inches in diameter.*

BUILDING BRIEF

Design and build a satellite that can orbit Earth. What it does is not so important—being the first one up in space is what it's all about!

Engineer: Sergei Korolev

Chief constructor: Mikhail S. Khomyakov

BEEP, BEEP

*The power for the tiny craft and radio **transmitter** came from three silver-zinc batteries.*

Sputnik 1 had four antennae that stuck out from the body of the satellite.

*The outer shell was made from polished **aluminum**, so that it could reflect sunlight and be seen from Earth.*

THE SPACE RACE

In July 1956, the United States announced that it was close to launching the first satellite into space. Russia, then part of the U.S.S.R., wanted to be the first country to explore space and had been planning to launch a big and heavy satellite. However, in order to beat the United States, they decided to quickly assemble something much smaller. As a result, *Sputnik 1* was launched on October 4, four months before the United State launched its first satellite, *Explorer 1*.

THE LAUNCH CRAFT

To get *Sputnik 1* into orbit, an enormous rocket, called *R-7*, was needed. Rocket engines burn large amounts of fuel and oxygen. The resulting high-pressure **exhaust** gas is released at the bottom, pushing the rocket off the ground and thrusting it into the air. It's like letting the air out of a balloon.

A rocket needs to travel more than 25,000 miles per hour to break away from the Earth's **gravitational pull**.

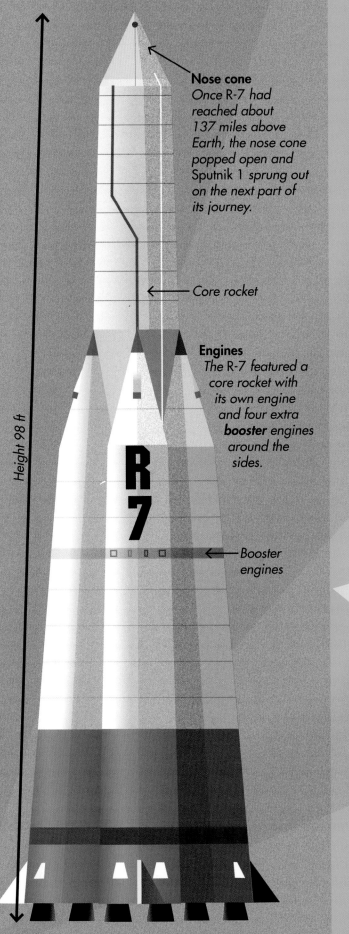

Nose cone
Once R-7 had reached about 137 miles above Earth, the nose cone popped open and Sputnik 1 sprung out on the next part of its journey.

← Core rocket

Engines
*The R-7 featured a core rocket with its own engine and four extra **booster** engines around the sides.*

R 7

Height 98 ft

← Booster engines

Sputnik 1 traveled around Earth for 92 days. Discoveries made and tested during the orbit were limited but important.

- The launch of *Sputnik 1* proved that spacecraft could be sent outside Earth's atmosphere and maintain an orbit.
- Scientists learned how **radio wave**s traveled back to Earth.
- Scientists could measure the **density** of the atmosphere as *Sputnik 1* traveled through it.

Sputnik 1 traveled at 18,000 mph and went around Earth 1,440 times. Each complete orbit took 98 minutes. When the batteries failed after three weeks, it slowed down, which caused it to eventually be pulled back down by Earth's gravity. It burned up in the atmosphere as it fell.

VOSTOK 1

The first human launched into space was Yuri Gagarin. He left Earth on April 12, 1961, on *Vostok 1*, a launch rocket that contained his capsule, *Vostok 3KA*. Once in space, the released capsule took 106 minutes to complete one historic orbit of Earth—up to 203 mi above the ground—before coming back down.

STAGE 1

BUILDING BRIEF

Launch a rocket capable of carrying a human into space, orbiting Earth, and then carrying him safely back home again. Also be the first country in the world to achieve this.

Space agency:
Soviet Space Program

Stage 1:
Four booster rockets burned their fuel up after two minutes, and then fell away.

Stage 2:
The core engine blazed for 30 seconds before being ejected.

Stage 3:
The remaining part of the craft sped on at 5 miles per second. It ejected the Vostok 3KA capsule into orbit 10 minutes into the flight.

VOSTOK 1

THE ROCKET

The *Vostok 1* rocket was similar in design to the *R-7*. It worked in three spectacular stages to thrust Gagarin and the Vostok 3KA space capsule into space.

Ejector seat hatch

Porthole

Ejector seat

GAGARIN'S VIEW

Gagarin was the first human to see Earth from outer space. Despite all the amazing technology and engineering wizardry, he had a simple paper notebook with a pencil tied to it to take notes.

3KA

Tanks hold nitrogen and oxygen. These are used for life support and to fuel the retro engine.

Retro engine

The Vostok 3KA capsule was controlled remotely from Earth because scientists were unsure if Gagarin would be able to move and think properly in the weightlessness of space.

BACK TO EARTH

To assist in bringing the capsule down to Earth, a retro rocket was fired in the opposite direction to the orbit path. This slowed the capsule down and helped it enter Earth's atmosphere.

Gagarin had to parachute out of the capsule at 4.3 mi above Earth. He landed in a field in Russia and was found by a lady and her granddaughter who had been working in their potato field.

SATURN V

The *Apollo 11* mission to take the first humans to the moon, launched in 1969. It used the *Saturn V* rocket, the command **module** *Columbia*, and the lunar module *Eagle* to get the astronauts into space, onto the moon, and safely back down to Earth.

SATURN V ROCKET

The success of the *Apollo 11* mission relied on the power of *Saturn V*. At the time, it was the tallest and heaviest rocket ever built. *Saturn V* worked in three stages:

Stage 1 had five F1 engines, featuring a single **combustion** chamber burning liquid fuel. This was the most powerful rocket engine ever built. When the fuel burned up, this section of *Saturn V* dropped away and Stage 2 began.

Stage 2 featured five J2 rocket engines. The engines burned liquid hydrogen and liquid oxygen. These fuels worked well in the higher atmosphere where it is colder. The atmosphere kept them in their liquid state, but it was not cold enough to freeze them.

Stage 3 had one J2 engine that fired once to put *Apollo 11* into a low Earth orbit then stopped. Once the Earth, moon, and spacecraft were in the correct positions, the engine fired again, taking *Columbia* and the *Eagle* to the moon.

STAGE 2

STAGE 1

Command module
Height: 10 ft
Diameter: 12 ft

Columbia finally came back down to Earth by parachute, splashing down in the ocean.

After the command module, Columbia, was freed from the stage 3 rocket, it turned to collect the lunar landing module on its nose.

Astronauts Buzz Aldrin and Neil Armstrong left for the moon in the lunar landing module, Eagle. Michael Collins stayed behind to control Columbia.

After exploring the moon, Aldrin and Armstrong got back into the Eagle, fired its rockets, and returned to the command module Columbia, leaving Eagle's landing legs on the moon. Once the men were all back in Columbia, the Eagle was pitched into space.

The outer layers of the command module were heavily **insulated** and included corkwood. These materials were designed to burn away in the intense 5,000°Fahrenheit temperatures experienced upon reentry into Earth's atmosphere. Back in Earth's atmosphere, the module fell toward Earth.

An astonishing 600 million people watched the historic moon landing on TV.

FUEL CELLS

Electric power for the spacecraft was provided by hydrogen and oxygen fuel cells. When hydrogen and oxygen mix in the cell, energy is released that can be converted to electric power. The clever part of this process is that mixing hydrogen and oxygen creates water—water that the astronauts were able to drink on the trip!

LUNAR ROVING VEHICLES

Nicknamed moon buggies, lunar roving vehicles (LRVs) were built for three of the Apollo space missions in 1971 and 1972. When the astronauts landed on the moon, they could drive around in the LRVs and explore a larger area.

BUILDING BRIEF

Design and build a vehicle to be driven on the moon. It must be strong enough to handle the lunar landscape.

Space agency: NASA

Location of abandoned vehicles:
Three Apollo moon buggies have been left behind on the moon.

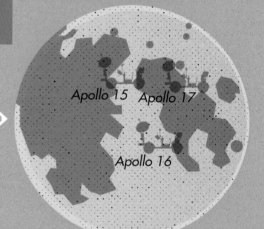

Apollo 15   Apollo 17

Apollo 16

STOWAWAY

The buggy was hidden away inside the wall of the lunar module. Once the lunar module landed on the moon, the buggy popped out, ready to rove!

1 *Astronauts pull hatch open.*

2 *As the hatch fully opens, the front wheels pop out first.*

3 *The rear wheels pop out as the hatch is lowered.*

4 *The astronauts pull the rover clear of the lunar module.*

LONGEST MOON BUGGY JOURNEYS

The LRV could only travel a short distance from the landing craft in case it broke down and the astronaut had to walk back.

LRV:	Longest single journey:
Apollo 15	7.75 mi
Apollo 16	7.20 mi
Apollo 17	12.50 mi

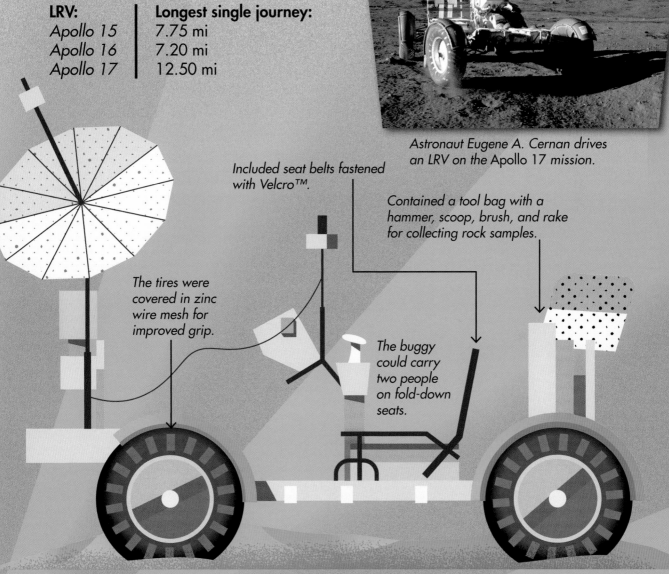

Astronaut Eugene A. Cernan drives an LRV on the Apollo 17 mission.

Included seat belts fastened with Velcro™.

Contained a tool bag with a hammer, scoop, brush, and rake for collecting rock samples.

The tires were covered in zinc wire mesh for improved grip.

The buggy could carry two people on fold-down seats.

Each of the four wheels had a battery-driven motor.

RUGGED ROVER

Lunar rover vehicles had to be super-tough to handle the bumpy, dusty surface and lightweight enough for the command module to carry them. The main frame was made from aluminum **alloy** tubing and weighed just 450 pounds. The exterior had to be able to withstand the extreme temperatures experienced in space, from −148°F to +248°F.

VOYAGER 1 AND VOYAGER 2

The *Voyager 1* and *Voyager 2* spacecrafts launched within a few days of each other aboard separate *Titan-Centaur* rockets. They set off in 1977 with a mission to fly further into space than any other spacecraft, right to the edge of the sun's reach and possibly beyond. They have been exploring space for more than 40 years and are still going strong.

BUILDING BRIEF

Build a craft that can journey far into space. It will need to collect information on the major planets then travel on for as long as it can, exploring the far reaches of the solar system and beyond.

Project scientist: Ed Stone

Space agency: NASA

It takes around 17 hours for signals from the Voyagers to get back to Earth.

VOYAGER TWINS

Voyager 1 and *Voyager 2* are identical. Their antennae are always pointing toward Earth so they can radio back their findings. They measure and collect various kinds of data, such as:

- the speed of solar winds
- magnetic fields
- **cosmic rays**.

Voyager 1 and *Voyager 2* each have a tiny amount of memory storage; the average mobile phone has 270,000 times more storage power. The signals they send also have a tiny amount of power—the same as a refrigerator lightbulb!

In 2017, Voyager 1 was 13 billion mi from the sun, and Voyager 2 was 11 billion mi from the sun.

MAIN MISSIONS

Each Voyager was tasked to fly past different planets and moons in our solar system.

Voyager 1's achievements:
- It flew past Jupiter and its moons, discovering volcanoes on the surface of the moon Io.
- It flew past Saturn and its moons, sending back images of icy surfaces on the moons. This proved that there is water elsewhere in the galaxy.
- It also took the first image of Earth and its moon together.

Voyager 2's achievements:
- It flew past Jupiter and Saturn and their moons.
- It sent back the first close-up images of Uranus and Neptune.
- It discovered there are rings around Uranus and found 10 new moons orbiting the planet.
- It found that Neptune has four rings and also discovered five new moons orbiting the planet.

Their next goal is to continue deeper into space on the Voyager Interstellar Mission (VIM). They will travel outside the **heliosphere**—the area of magnetic force from the sun, going through the **heliosheath** boundary and on to **interstellar space**.

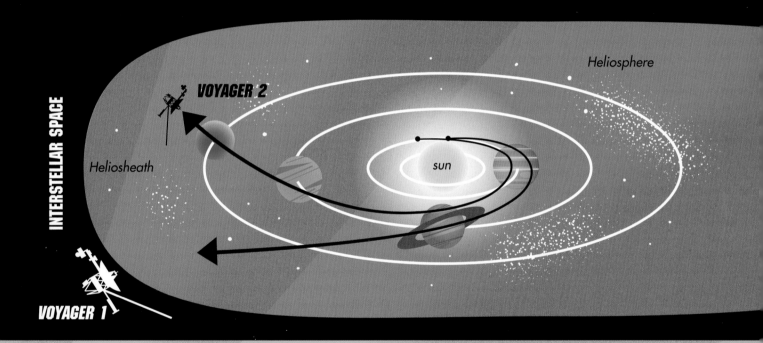

INTERSTELLAR SPACE

Heliosphere

VOYAGER 2

Heliosheath

sun

VOYAGER 1

POWER SOURCE

Although their journey has been the longest of any spacecraft in history, the Voyagers have amazingly little power. Power is supplied by three generators. These use **thermocouples**—two pieces of wire made of different metals that are heated by the radioactive metal **plutonium**. They metals warm at different temperatures, which produces a spark between the wires that is converted into electric power. It's a source of power that needs no moveable parts. They will generate power until 2020. After then, the Voyagers will drift in space on the same course.

THERMOCOUPLE

← Electric power

Metal 1

Metal 2

Heat released by the radioactive decay of plutonium

SPACE SHUTTLE

The first space shuttle, launched in 1981, was a feat of technical genius. It was a spacecraft that was not only reusable, but it could take off like a rocket and land like an aircraft! The space shuttle was also the first winged spacecraft to orbit Earth.

BUILDING BRIEF

Build a reusable spacecraft to enable the launch of future space missions and the construction of a space station.

Space agency: NASA

LIFTOFF

The orange external tank (ET) fed fuel to the shuttle's main engines, while the solid rocket boosters (SRBs) strapped to the side provided additional thrust. The SRBs fired until the shuttle reached an height of 28 mi above the ground. Then they detached and fell to Earth using parachutes and were recovered for future use. At this point, the nearly empty tank separated and fell in a preplanned path with the majority of it disintegrating in the atmosphere and the rest falling into the ocean.

It took 8.5 minutes for the space shuttle, called an orbiter, to reach space. Once there, it powered itself with its own fuel and engines.

The huge external fuel tank used to be painted white. But this added extra weight, so they decided to leave it in its original color—bright orange!

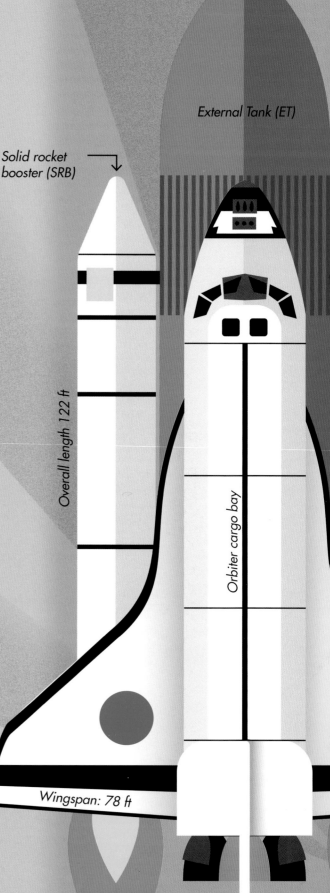

External Tank (ET)

Solid rocket booster (SRB)

Overall length 122 ft

Orbiter cargo bay

Wingspan: 78 ft

CANADARM

Canadarm was the shuttle's robotic arm system; it was 50 ft long and had six joints to imitate the movement of a human arm. Extending out from the orbiter cargo bay and controlled by computer, it was used for lifting, climbing, grabbing satellites out of the sky, and even tapping ice off the outside of the orbiter on frosty days!

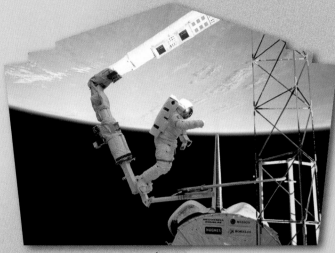

Canadarm in action

LOOPY LANDING

The orbiter had to start preparing to land halfway around Earth from where it landed. It needed that much distance to slow down. During descent, it flipped over to fly upside down, firing retro rockets backward to slow it down. It flipped in the air and descended at a 40-degree angle through the atmosphere. Once it reached the runway, a parachute opened to slow it down.

40°

Turning from side to side helped slow the shuttle before landing.

MOVEABLE ENGINE NOZZLES

The space shuttle had three exhaust nozzles where the gases from the burning fuel escaped. This gas pushed the rocket forward. The nozzles were moveable, which allowed the orbiter to use the force of the gas to help steer and control the direction in which it traveled. They moved on a gimbal, a device that has a fixed axis with circles that rotate around, allowing for controlled movement of the engines when the rocket is moving and shaking.

Fixed axis

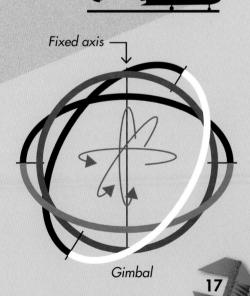

Gimbal

HUBBLE SPACE TELESCOPE

The Hubble Space Telescope was launched from the space shuttle *Discovery* in 1990. It orbits at 340 mi above Earth's surface and travels at an incredible 17,000 mph. Hubble has sent back amazing images that have changed the way we think about space.

BUILDING BRIEF

Design a telescope that can work in space with a super-strong lens that can record images free from the distractions of light and weather.

Space agency: NASA

CASSEGRAIN REFLECTOR

Hubble is a Cassegrain **reflector** telescope, meaning that it has two mirrors inside it—one **convex** and one **concave**. These reflect and intensify the outside view then direct it to an on-board computer. The glass of the main concave mirror had to be polished for two years before the aluminum backing was added to turn it into a mirror.

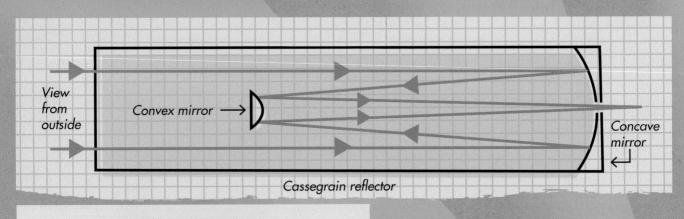

View from outside

Convex mirror →

Concave mirror ←

Cassegrain reflector

DATA TRANSFER

Hubble's data makes a complicated journey back to Earth. It goes from the Hubble computer via its transmitter to a space satellite. A giant receiver dish on the ground in New Mexico moves to track the satellite and picks up the signal. From there, the data goes to the Goddard Space Flight Center near Washington, D.C. After that, the data goes to the Hubble headquarters at the Space Telescope Science Institute in Baltimore, Maryland, where the information is stored and analyzed.

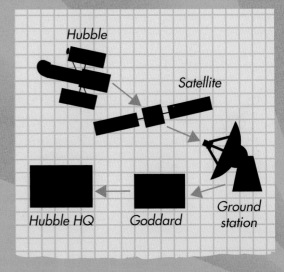

Hubble

Satellite

Hubble HQ   Goddard   Ground station

Outside view enters here

High gain antenna →

The telescope is named after astronomer Edwin Hubble. He discovered that there were galaxies outside the Milky Way and proved that the Universe is expanding.

There was a defect on the telescope mirror when it was first launched. Astronauts from the space shuttle had to add moving mirrors to help the focus, like a giant pair of eyeglasses!

Hubble can see so clearly so far into space that it's like being in the United States and being able to see a butterfly in Japan!

Solar panel

Anyone can apply to use the telescope by contacting NASA with a proposal of what they would like to look for.

← Solar panel

Low gain antenna for receiving commands from Earth.

High gain antenna sends data back to Earth.

SPECTACULAR HUBBLE SNAPSHOTS

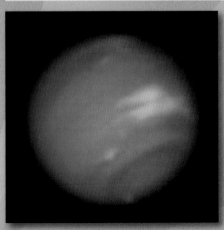

A shot of Neptune showing light and dark vortex clouds.

The death of a star forming the Calabash **Nebula**.

Pillars of gas and dust as stars are created in the Carina Nebula.

19

ROSETTA SPACE PROBE

The *Rosetta* space probe was launched in 2004 as part of a 10-year mission to follow and study a comet called 67P/Churyumov-Gerasimenko. The probe was looking for signs of life on comets and other planets.

BUILDING BRIEF

Design and build a spacecraft that can chase and study a comet across thousands of miles, carrying a small lander that will ultimately end up on the moving comet.

Space agency: European Space Agency

Solar panels

ORBIT ADVENTURE

The *Rosetta* probe was a small aluminum box with wings covered in solar cells that provided its power. This tiny craft traveled for 10 years in a complex series of orbits that helped it gain speed and the right position to catch its comet. It had to go around the sun three times, gathering speed from the gravity on Earth and Mars to then gain a larger orbit.

The Rosetta *space probe had to reach speeds of 34,000 mph to travel alongside the 67P comet. When it did, it took amazing photos of the surface.*

Rosetta

Comet

sun

1 2 3

Mars

Earth

EXPERIMENTS

The *Rosetta* probe, along with its landing module, *Philae*, ran 11 different experiments. Among other things, they analyzed temperatures, atmosphere, and gravity and collected dust and gases. *Rosetta* found oxygen, nitrogen, and the **amino acid** glycine—an organic compound that could have brought life to planets.

The experiment instruments were set on top of Rosetta so they could catch information from the speeding comet.

← Philae *lander*

PHILAE LANDER

The small robotic *Philae* lander was released from *Rosetta* and landed on the comet on November 12, 2014. It was an enormous technical achievement. It didn't land in a perfect position, but it did manage to send back images and data about the surface rock.

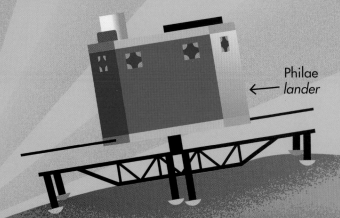

Philae ← lander

In 2016, Rosetta purposely crashed into the comet because its power was failing.

INTERNATIONAL SPACE STATION

The *International Space Station (ISS)* is the only permanently inhabited craft in space and is an amazing example of what can be achieved by combining the technical talents and expertise of many nations.

BUILDING BRIEF

Design and build a space station in which people can live and work together for long periods of time in zero gravity.

Space agency: NASA and 14 other national agencies

GIANT SPACE JIGSAW

The *ISS* is a giant floating science laboratory in space. It was put together in space. Construction began in 1998 when the first piece was put into orbit during a Russian mission. It took more than 115 space flights to deliver the rest of the components and build the *ISS*. It contains many modules that fit together like a giant jigsaw puzzle. These contain laboratories, a bathroom, and everything else the crew needs, including a fitness area!

LEARNING LAB

So much has been studied and learned aboard the *ISS*. Some of the experiments have included:

- growing plants
- studying fire
- studying the effects of living in zero gravity
- observing **dark matter** and cosmic rays
- observing changes in Earth's atmosphere.

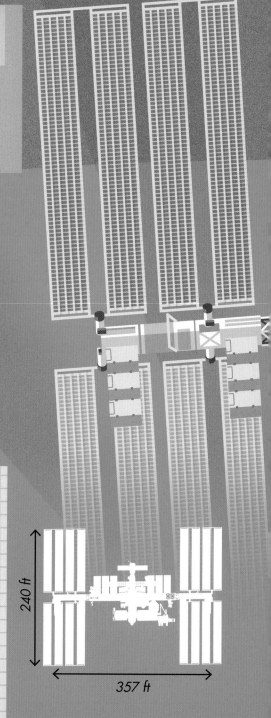

240 ft

357 ft

SUCCESSFUL SPACE SHAPES

The *ISS* is made up of many different shaped components all designed to be the best shape and structure for their job.

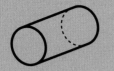

The modules where the astronauts live and work are cylinders or spheres. Like a soda can, these are shapes that are good for a pressurized interior.

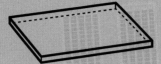

The panels holding the solar cells are flat and wide to collect as much power from the sun as possible.

The central modules and solar panels are connected by a strong backbone made from a network of triangular **latticed titanium**, called a truss. Lattice structures are used on bridges because of their structural strength.

The ISS orbits 250 mi above Earth.

CUPOLA

One of the modules, the **cupola**, is used for observation and sits on the Earth-facing side of the *ISS*. The cupola gives an all-round view of incoming crafts and outside operations. It's the control center for the **manipulator arm** that is used for loading and unloading cargo, catching and repairing satellites, and anchoring astronauts who are working outside.

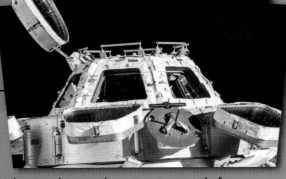

The cupola's windowpanes are made from specially strengthened glass and have shutters to protect them from flying space debris.

WILKINSON MICROWAVE ANISOTROPY PROBE

The *Wilkinson Microwave Anisotropy Probe (WMAP)* was an awesome small craft that, until 2010, scanned the sky looking for clues to answer big questions, such as how old is the universe? What is it made from? How has it changed? And the answers are amazing!

BUILDING BRIEF

Design and build a spacecraft to reach an orbit that can look into deep space to find cosmic **radiation** left over from the beginning of the universe.

Space agency: NASA with Johns Hopkins and Princeton University

CENTRIPETAL ORBIT

WMAP was launched in 2001 with a complex looping journey to help it gain enough speed to swing out toward a distant region of space called Lagrange 2. At this point in space, its orbit was not around a planet, but like the end of a swinging **pendulum** instead. This is called a **centripetal** orbit. *WMAP* used the gravitational force of Earth, the moon, and the sun to achieve this orbit.

WMAP faced away from the sun and scanned outward, looking for heat remaining from the beginning of the universe. As it orbited, the front moved around so it could scan 360 degrees at a time.

Lunar orbit

WMAP orbit

0.9 million mi

Size 15.7 ft x 11.8 ft

Gregorian optics and separate reflectors

Sight

Spin direction

Sight

Centripetal orbit

Solar panels faced toward the sun, while WMAP's umbrella shape shaded the equipment from the sun's rays.

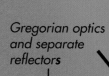

SKY SCANNER

WMAP used two back-to-back **Gregorian telescopes** that scanned for cosmic microwave background radiation, recorded as temperature. Taking two sets of information at a time meant they could be compared. Readings were channeled into the telescopes by reflectors and then bounced back and forth on the mirrors inside to magnify them.

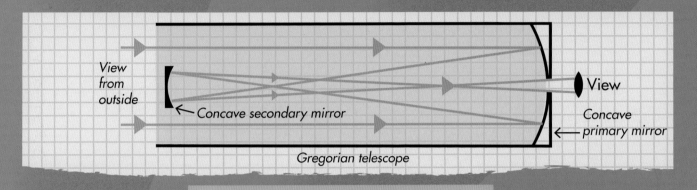

View from outside

←—Concave secondary mirror

View

Concave primary mirror →

Gregorian telescope

DYNAMIC DISCOVERIES

WMAP made amazing discoveries. This tiny machine was able to date the universe to when it began: 13.77 billion years ago! It also drew a map of the universe from its beginning to now. This showed that the universe is expanding and that the rate of expansion is speeding up.

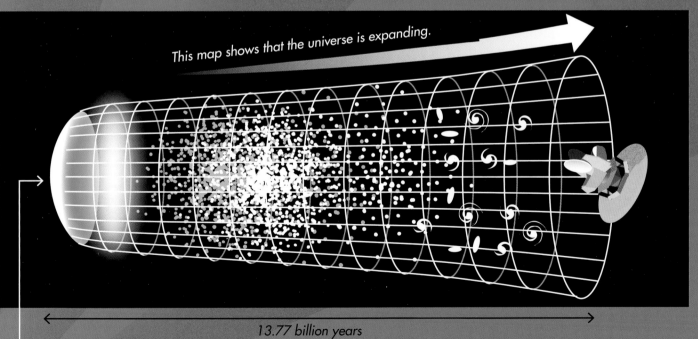

This map shows that the universe is expanding.

←———— *13.77 billion years* ————→

The map shows the point at which stars started to shine, which was when the universe was about 500 million years old!

It also shows what the universe is made of: 4.6 percent atoms, 24 percent dark matter, and 71.4 percent **dark energy**.

SPIRIT AND OPPORTUNITY MARS ROVERS

Robotic explorers named *Spirit* and *Opportunity* were sent to Mars in 2003. The rovers' mission was to study Martian **geology**. To do this, they rolled for mile after mile across the surface of the planet examining rocks and minerals along the way.

BUILDING BRIEF

Design and build planet explorers to search the surface of Mars, collecting rocks and hunting for evidence of water.

Space agency: NASA

ROCKER-BOGIE

The surface of Mars is very rocky, so each rover uses a special device called a rocker-bogie that helps them tackle rough terrain without shaking the rover's body too much.

Moveable arms connected to the wheels allow them all to stay on the ground. The rocking motion of the wheels actually helps keep the instruments on top steady as the rovers move.

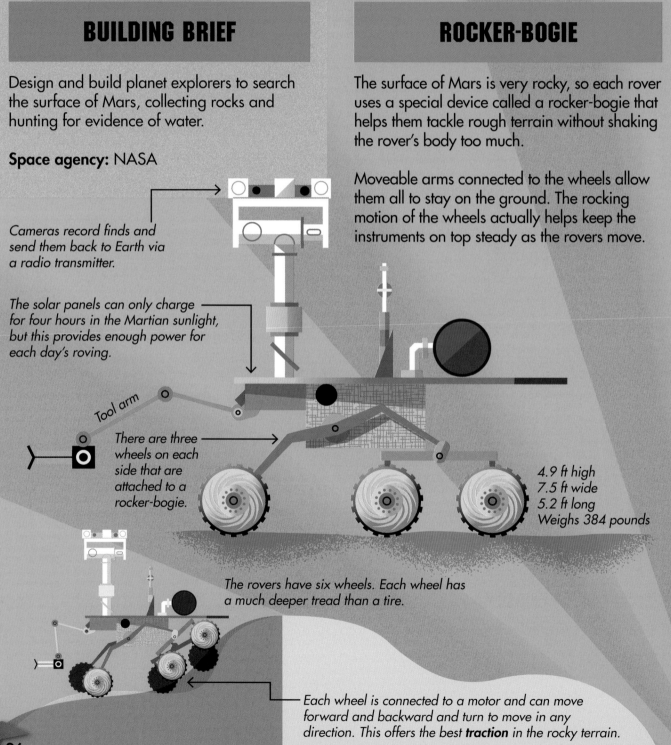

Cameras record finds and send them back to Earth via a radio transmitter.

The solar panels can only charge for four hours in the Martian sunlight, but this provides enough power for each day's roving.

Tool arm

There are three wheels on each side that are attached to a rocker-bogie.

4.9 ft high
7.5 ft wide
5.2 ft long
Weighs 384 pounds

The rovers have six wheels. Each wheel has a much deeper tread than a tire.

*Each wheel is connected to a motor and can move forward and backward and turn to move in any direction. This offers the best **traction** in the rocky terrain.*

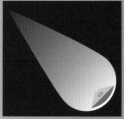

Capsule enters Mars' atmosphere

Parachute and retro rockets slow capsule

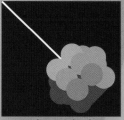

Airbags deploy

Rover lands and bounces

Airbags deflate and rover opens

Ready to go!

CRASH LANDING

The rovers were launched into space in June and July of 2003. It took less than seven months for them to reach their orbit around Mars.

The mission needed to follow a careful process to deliver the rovers safely to the Martian surface. First, a parachute and a stiff heat shield called an aeroshell were used to slow the rovers down as they fell toward Mars. Retro rockets were also fired to make them go even slower. Airbags were inflated to cushion the rovers as they landed. Once they had bounced to a halt, the airbags deflated. Finally, the rovers' legs, called petals, were designed to open up in such a way that the rovers would always land upright. Once the rovers had charged their solar-powered batteries, they were ready to start their Martian missions!

FINDINGS

The rovers sent pictures back to Earth via a radio transmitter. Among their important discoveries were magnetic dust, meteorites, and evidence of water. *Spirit* ended communications in 2010, but *Opportunity* keeps on rolling!

The image above was taken by Opportunity in March 2015. It shows the surface of Mars and a large crater that scientists named Spirit of St. Louis Crater in honor of Charles Lindbergh, who in 1927 became the first person to fly nonstop across the Atlantic Ocean in his airplane, the Spirit of St. Louis.

FASCINATING FACTS

Spacecraft and space exploration have inspired many engineering inventions. But did you know how many have been adapted for use on Earth?

Many smartphone cameras use digital technology that was invented by NASA for use on space missions.

Joysticks can be used to play video games, but they were first used to steer lunar roving vehicles.

NASA developed cordless drills for collecting moon samples on the Apollo missions.

TRAVEL DISTANCES OF CRAFT

New Horizons space probe was launched in 2007. Its main goal was to fly to Pluto to send back information on the dwarf planet that was still unexplored at the time. It sent back amazing photos and is now heading toward its next destination in the **Kuiper Belt**. It is currently about 3.6 billion miles from Earth.

1 2 3 4 5 6 7

Billion miles from the Earth

Cochlear implants are devices for hearing invented by Kennedy Space Center engineer Adam Kissiah, who worked on the space shuttle program. A microphone sends signals to an implant in the patient's ear to restore or enhance hearing.

Sneaker soles are now formed using a process called blow rubber molding that was first used to create moon boots for an Apollo mission.

Solar cells were not invented for use on space missions, but they are vital for powering spacecraft. For this reason, space agencies have invested in solar-cell technology to make them more and more efficient. This improves spacecraft and life on Earth.

Pioneer 11, which launched in 1973, flew past Saturn and sent back pictures revealing two new moons and another ring. Right now, it's about 9.1 billion miles from Earth.

Pioneer 10, which launched in 1972, flew to Jupiter and then beyond. It was the first spacecraft to fly through the **asteroid belt**, and it sent signals back for 30 years.

Voyager 2

Voyager 1

9 10 11 12 13 14 15

Billion miles from Earth

READ MORE

Carson, Mary Kay. *Mission to Pluto: The First Visit to an Ice Dwarf and the Kuiper Belt.* Scientists in the Field. Boston: Houghton Mifflin Harcourt, 2016.

Green, Jen. *The Story of the Race to the Moon.* Explorers. Mankato, Minn.: Book House, 2017.

Owen, Ruth. *Spacecraft.* Objects in Space. New York: Powerkids Press, 2015.

Rowell, Rebecca. *Building Rockets.* Engineering Challenges. Mendota Heights, Minn.: North Star Editions, 2017.

Rusch, Elizabeth. *The Mighty Mars Rovers: The Incredible Adventures of* Spirit *and* Opportunity. Scientists in the Field. St. Louis, Mo.: Turtleback Books, 2017.

INTERNET SITES

Use Facthound to find Internet sites related to this book.
Just type in 9781543513370 and go!

Check out projects, games and lots more at
www.capstonekids.com

GLOSSARY

alloy a substance made by melting and mixing two or more metals with another substance

amino acids the basic building blocks of protein

asteroid belt the area in space between Mars and Jupiter where the most asteroids are found

booster a rocket or engine that gives extra power to a spacecraft

centripetal pulling an object turning in a circle inward toward the center

combustion the process of catching fire and burning

comet a ball of rock and ice that circles the sun

communication the sharing of information

concave curved inward, like the inside of a bowl

convex curved outward, like the outside of a ball

cosmic rays particles that bombard Earth from anywhere beyond its atmosphere

cupola a rounded roof or ceiling

dark energy a form of energy that scientists can't detect but they believe is out in space that produces a force that opposes gravity

dark matter invisible matter that scientists can't detect but they believe is out in space

density the relationship of an object's mass to its volume

ejector seat a seat that can propel the sitter safely out of a spacecraft or airplane in an emergency

exhaust the waste gases produced by an engine

galaxy a group of stars and planets

geology the study of how Earth was formed and how it changes

gravitational pull the pulling force of gravity

gravity a force that pulls objects with mass together; gravity pulls objects down toward the center of Earth

Gregorian telescope a type of telescope invented in the 17th century that has two concave mirrors inside it

insulate to cover with a material to protect from extreme temperatures

interstellar space in our solar system, the place in space beyond the magnetic field of the sun

Kuiper Belt the area of the solar system beyond Neptune

lattice a pattern formed by strips of material that cross each other diagonally

lunar having to do with a moon

manipulator arm a robotic arm

microwave a short radio wave between one millimeter and one meter in wavelength

module a separate section that can be linked to other parts

nebula a huge, bright cloud of gas and dust found in space

pendulum a weight that swings back and forth from a fixed point

plutonium a radioactive metallic element

radiation rays of energy given off by certain elements

radio waves invisible waves that carry sounds and images through the air

reflector a shiny surface that bounces back light

satellite an object used for communicating or collecting information that moves around Earth in space

solar cell a device that turns sunlight into energy

solar panel a group of solar cells that absorb sunlight and change it into electrical energy

spherical having a solid round form like that of a basketball or globe

technology the use of science to do practical things, such as designing complex machines

thermocouple a device for measuring temperature in which a pair of wires of different metals are joined

thruster an engine that pushes a vehicle forward (thrusts) by discharging fluid or particles

titanium a light, strong metal found in various minerals that is used to make steel

traction the amount of grip one surface has while moving over another surface

transmitter a device that sends out radio signals

INDEX